PAMPHLETS ON AMERICAN WRITERS · NUMBER 95

UNIVERSITY OF MINNESOTA

James Agee

BY ERLING LARSEN

UNIVERSITY OF MINNESOTA PRESS · MINNEAPOLIS

Printed in the United States of America at
the North Central Publishing Company, St. Paul

Library of Congress Catalog Card Number: 78-633324
ISBN 0-8166-0599-8

The excerpt from "Draft Lyrics for Candide" is reproduced
from *The Collected Poems of James Agee*, edited by Robert
Fitzgerald, by permission of the publisher, Houghton Mifflin
Company. Part of this pamphlet first appeared, in a different
form, in the *Carleton Miscellany* and is used
with the permission of the journal.

PUBLISHED IN GREAT BRITAIN, INDIA, AND PAKISTAN BY THE OXFORD
UNIVERSITY PRESS, LONDON, BOMBAY, AND KARACHI, AND IN CANADA
BY THE COPP CLARK PUBLISHING CO. LIMITED, TORONTO

JAMES AGEE

ERLING LARSEN is a professor of English at Carleton College and was for a number of years the editor of the *Carleton Miscellany*. He is the author of many short stories, essays, and reviews and two books, *Minnesota Trails: A Sentimental History* and *Something about Some of the Educations of Laird Bell.*

↗ *James Agee*

ON MAY 16, 1955, while riding in a taxicab on his way to a doctor's office, James Agee died of a heart attack. Two days later, the *New York Times* ran his obituary. With the photograph that appeared next to the headline, the whole took up about three-fourths of a column. It included a brief summary of Agee's career as poet, critic, novelist, reporter, and writer of movie scripts. It mentioned three books: *Permit Me Voyage*, the volume of youthful verse; *Let Us Now Praise Famous Men*, the account of a sojourn among the tenant farmers of Alabama; *The Morning Watch*, a short novel about life at an Episcopal school in the South. It quoted excerpts from one review of each of these books. Those concerning the poetry and the novel were kind. That concerning *Let Us Now Praise Famous Men* described the book as "arrogant, mannered, precious, gross." About two weeks later, in its issue dated May 30, *Time* printed an obituary in its "Milestones" section. It was six lines long.

With no other evidence than these obituaries, one would assume that Agee had achieved no great literary fame. Of course, he died as a comparatively young man and his output had been small. Further, many of his years had been spent in near anonymity as a reporter and editor for *Fortune* and as a critic for *Time*. Still, his signed output, his "own work" as he frequently called it, had been widely reviewed, and Agee had friends and admirers who were certain they could recognize his hand in whatever he wrote however anonymously.

It is true, though, that Agee's greatest fame came posthumously.

It began to grow when he was awarded the Pulitzer Prize in 1957 for his novel *A Death in the Family*. It increased during the next three years as his movie reviews were gathered and published in a celebration of the intellectuals' new interest in what they now called "film." In 1960 *Let Us Now Praise Famous Men* was reprinted. Since then, three volumes of Agee's work have been published: one containing his collected poetry, another his collected shorter prose, and a third the letters he wrote to his teacher and friend Father James Harold Flye. The letters, frank and intimate, cast invaluable light on the life and the nature of the man who wrote them. They are certainly among Agee's most important writings.

James Rufus Agee was born on November 27, 1909, in Knoxville, Tennessee. His father, Hugh James Agee, died in 1916. In 1919 his mother took for the summer a cottage near the campus of Saint Andrew's, a grade and high school directed by members of the Order of the Holy Cross, a monastic order of the Episcopal Church. Mrs. Agee eventually decided to stay at Saint Andrew's (which was near enough to Knoxville for frequent visits) so that her children, James Rufus and his sister Emma, might attend the school. Among the teachers was Father Flye. Agee was to find his major literary themes in the death of his father, in the life of the Knoxville family, in the intellectual concerns that he shared with Father Flye, and in the social and religious attitudes of the Saint Andrew's community.

The correspondence with Father Flye started when Agee entered Phillips Exeter Academy shortly before his sixteenth birthday. In October of 1925 he wrote that his literary life had begun. "I have written stuff for the *Monthly*, and I am to get a story and 2 or 3 poems in this month. This will get me into the Lantern Club, I hope. That is one of the big things to be in here. It runs the *Monthly*, and is a literary club." In 1927 he was elected editor of the *Monthly* and president of the Lantern Club. From Exeter he went to Harvard, where he became president of the *Advocate*.

In his letters he gave a running account of his very wide reading, and he was usually careful to steer a middle course in his criticisms. *Elmer Gantry* was "disappointing, although excellent in spots." *Manhattan Transfer* was "an unalleviatedly filthy book . . . [but] full of lovely descriptions." And not only did he read, but he met and corresponded with various established writers. S. Foster Damon even read one of Agee's poems and said "he thought [it] was good"; he gave Agee the names of others to whom he might show his work. Among them was Robert Frost, who "said even better things" about it than had Damon. At Harvard, Agee came under the influence of I. A. Richards, "altogether the most important thing in that spring [of 1931]." Richards "thinks my poetry good — maybe more than good."

Such judgments on his work no doubt reinforced Agee's wavering determination to become a writer, and he clearly needed whatever moral support he could get. Letters from his years at school and college show him torn and uncertain, enduring periods of sterility caused by failures in attempts obviously too ambitious, wanting above all to become a writer but not knowing what he wanted to write, neglecting his schoolwork in order to write and then deciding he would never be more than a minor poet. At times he was "conscious of a gradual spiritual and ethical atrophy," but in his junior year at Harvard he experienced "the most extraordinary and grand 3 months" of his life, working on the *Advocate* and busy with "courses, reading, my own writing, tutorial reading. . . . Everything going *continuously* at top speed — mind, body and nerves; and with an intensity I've never known before."

Nor was he to escape these changes in mood during his later life. After graduating from Harvard and going to work on *Fortune* he "felt like suicide for weeks . . . and not just fooling with the idea,

7

but feeling seriously on the edge of it." That was August 14, 1932. By August 18, however, he was "a lot better" and working hard.

The publication of his first book did not solve his problems. He wrote to Father Flye: "I am in most possible kinds of pain, mental and spiritual that is. In this pain the book and its contents are a relatively small item, only noticeable in the general unpleasantness because they are tangible. The rest of the trouble is even more inexpressable, and a lot more harm, but revolves chiefly around the simple-sounding problem of how to become what I wish I could when I can't. That, however, is fierce and complicated enough to keep me balancing over suicide as you might lean out over the edge of a high building, as far as you could and keep from falling but with no special or constant desire not to fall." The solution, "the wise answer . . . would be that there is only one coordinator and guide, and that he is come at through self-negation. But: that can mean nothing to me until or unless I learn it for myself. . . . There is much to enjoy and more to be glad for than I deserve, and I know it, but they are mostly, by my own difficulty, out of my reach."

Permit Me Voyage was published in 1934, a little more than two years after Agee's graduation from Harvard. The poems in the book vary in quality, perhaps inevitably: the earliest poem was written while Agee was still at Exeter and the latest were composed in the year of publication. The earliest, "Ann Garner," is a longish narrative poem that derives in manner and matter from the work of Robert Frost. The latest show that Agee had worked with increasing interest in and skill in using traditional Elizabethan and Jacobean forms. Nothing in the volume would then or now be considered "modern" or revolutionary. And the entire collection shows a bent toward literature, its sources being in literature rather than in current affairs or in Agee's daily life as journalist and observer.

This is not to say that the poetry is neither personal nor expres-

8

sive. Indeed, it is very personal. But it voices personality in an abstract and lofty way, in sustained flights high above the mundane. And some of the poems in their lushness of language and in their mannered rhetoric anticipate some of the more tortured parts of *Let Us Now Praise Famous Men.* The abstracted tone rises from the nature of the subject common to the greater number of the poems, a very deep concern for matters of religion and the spiritual life. Robert Fitzgerald, who edited *The Collected Poems of James Agee,* writes in his introduction that *Permit Me Voyage* evidences a "preparation of spirit."

The "Dedication" of *Permit Me Voyage* appears not at the beginning of the volume but after an opening section composed of "lyrics" and "songs." It is eight pages long, written in a King James kind of prose, and its tone shifts from one of solemn dedication to one of diatribe and finally of prayer. Agee dedicates the book, the poetry, and by implication the poet himself "in much humility to God in the highest in the trust that he despises nothing." He proceeds as if he were trying to list all the influences upon his life, and he succeeds in pointing to what were to be his continuing major literary interests. He dedicates the book to Christ and Van Gogh and Charles Spencer Chaplin, to his "brave father" James Agee and to "those unremembered who have died in no glory of peace," to "my land and to the squatters upon it," and to "Leopold Bloom, and in his mildheartedness to all mankind." He dedicates the book even to those who cause war and who profit from it but he takes pleasure in calling down punishment upon them. May their "loins thaw with a shrieking pain . . . to the sweet entertainment of all men of good will." And he ends with a prayer that God will "make the eyes of our hearts, and the voice of our hearts in speech, honest and lovely within the fences of our nature, and a little clear."

Although Agee never put together for publication another volume of verse, he was to continue writing poetry. *The Collected*

Poems makes a volume of 179 pages. Among the poems is "John Carter," a long Byronic satire which the poet worked on for at least four years but never completed. The collection also contains poems that show Agee's abiding assumption that poetry (and prose, for that matter) is essentially music — "Theme with Variations," for example. A number of poems are on religious subjects and one of them combines religion with Agee's Tennessee origins — "Lines Suggested by a Tennessee Song" tells in a mountain-ballad manner of the Annunciation of the Virgin and of the birth of Her Son. Others show a growing concern about "politics and economics" — "Two Songs on the Economy of Abundance," "Period Pieces from the Mid-Thirties," and so forth. And the volume concludes with "Draft Lyrics for *Candide*," written in 1954. This *Candide* was a comic operetta, with book by Lillian Hellman and score by Leonard Bernstein, for which Agee was called upon to write some lyrics (none of them finally used). In a sequence entitled "Love Poet" the last stanzas read:

> See how Love takes
> Man's true measure:
>
> Man's true hope begins:
> Head to hold us:
> Heart to bring us:
> One, in Love's sane hand.

Agee submitted these lyrics with a note that mentions the "preachiness problem" they raise. He concludes: "To preach seems valid and obligatory."

In his short stories, too, Agee frequently preached. Or, if he did not preach, he tried to put into the stories messages, more or less hidden, about religious and philosophic problems. He did not write many short stories, however. Most of them appeared very early. One of the earliest, printed in the *Advocate* of December 1929, when Agee was a sophomore at Harvard, is called "A Walk before Mass." It is not an easy story, being in part perhaps deliberately murky and obscure. It begins with a Hemingway trick — "He awoke at a little after four, and knew it was upon him again." The next two sentences point to the later Agee addiction to photographic precision: "It was scarcely daylight, and rain was dropping out of a bare sky. He watched blades of water delicately overlap and riffle down the pane." And a sentence near the end prefigures the later overblown rhetoric: "For a few seconds he stood motionless, arms above his head, flayed eyes fixed on the water."

The story is a trifle melodramatic. We soon learn that the "it" of the first sentence is the man's awareness of his inability to "bear" living with his wife. The only thing that keeps him from bolting is a young son, and we learn that at least once before the man had wished the son "had never been born . . . or were out of the way." On this rainy morning the man tries to pray. "O God, deliver my wife out of her iniquity. . . . Blessed is the fruit of thy womb, Jesus." He gets out of bed and goes to little Jerome, asks him to dress, tells him that they "must go for a walk." Together they go down to the bank of the river, to the place where the man first had wished the death of the boy. He wants to confess this to the boy and then go with him to Confession and Mass. But when he begins to speak, "My dear, my beloved son," he catches the boy up and hurls him into the water. It is then that we see the man's "flayed eyes fixed on the water."

The story presents difficulties. We know that the wife's name is Mary, but we are in some doubt about the nature of her "iniquity." We know that the son's initial is J and we assume that his death will free the man from his bondage to his wife. But remorse *may* hinder him. And we are in the final sentence presented with a number of symbolic difficulties when the man clenches his fists and strikes himself on the temple so hard that he has to lean against an elm.

Trees and temples, indeed. But we do wrong to jest about what is clearly a very serious youthful work and one dealing with problems Agee was to wrestle with all during his life. If we simplistically reduce the theme of the story to a vague generality — man's fear and awe and wonder in the face of the apparent gratuitousness and the inevitability of death and its effect upon the living — we can argue that the theme of this early story is the same as that of the last one, "A Mother's Tale," and of *A Death in the Family*.

Of these works, "A Mother's Tale" comes closest to failure. It is marked not by the vagueness of "A Walk before Mass" but by a great piling up of very specific detail about a matter that in lesser hands than Agee's could have been utterly incredible and verged upon silliness. The tale is not about a mother but one told by a mother who is a cow. Most of what we learn in the story we learn through the mother's words, addressed to the young calves around her. Agee in the role of omniscient narrator enters the story only briefly at the beginning and the end.

When the story opens, one calf had run up the hill to the cow. " 'Mama!' he cried out, all out of breath. 'What *is* it! What are they *doing*! Where are they *going*!' " The author describes what has caused this curiosity, "an immense drove of cattle" being moved across the plains, dogs yelping at them, men on horseback shouting, but only "tinily audible above a low and awesome sound which seemed to come not from the multitude of hooves but from the center of the world." Then, in answering the further questions of the young, the mother explains that the herd is going "away." The young are interested. "Where are they going?" The mother says she is not sure. The young keep pressing her until she finally admits, "There was one who came back. . . . Or so they say." The young "gathered a little more closely around her, for now she spoke very quietly," and we realize that we are in the midst of a small bovine epic. " 'It was my great-grandmother who told me,' she said. 'She was told it by *her* great-grandmother, who claimed she saw it with her own eyes, though of course I can't vouch for that.' " And the mother launches into her long story of the one who had returned and "told it all in a rush, they say, the last things first and every which way, but as it was finally sorted out and gotten into order by those who heard it and those they told it to, this is more or less what happened."

She describes the crowded cattle cars, the sudden jerks as the train advances and stops again for the loading of another car, the fright among the cattle, the "sudden and terrible scream" of the locomotive, the great speed when the train finally departs, the terror when the train goes around curves, the many stops at which the cattle hope for food and water but are given none, the great noise on the sidings as the cattle train waits for another train to pass. She tells "with a certain pleased vindictiveness" about the meeting with a train "as full of human beings as the car he was in was full of our kind."

From this point the story insists upon that analogy to human experience and even develops an analogy to man's making of myths and religious systems. When the cattle are finally released from the train they are moved to wonder by the beauty of the white fences in the stockyards and to fear by the smells that come from the slaughterhouse. They debate their situation, some thinking that the whole experience is a bad dream and others arguing that after their suffering and pain it is only right they should have earned their way into this new bliss, for they are now eating and drinking well and are among their own kind.

The hero, however, almost forgets this tribal unity or identity when he is being driven up the increasingly narrow corridors leading into the slaughterhouse. He takes pride in being a "creature separate and different from any other" and assumes he is going to some even greater reward when suddenly he looks up and sees on a bridge above him The Man With The Hammer. The hero emerges from unconsciousness hanging by the tendons of his heels while knives slice between his skin and his flesh. With a super-bull effort he tears himself loose from the hooks, charges past the knife-wielding men, breaks out of the slaughterhouse, and starts back to the West.

After an agonizing journey he reaches the ranch and calls the cattle together. He is a terrifying sight; his hooves buckle under him, the mark of the hammer is deep in his forehead, his skin flaps loose to expose his muscles. But when he begins to tell his fellows about Man's ultimate purpose many of them doubt his word and wonder whether anyone in his right mind would suffer so for others, and to still their doubts he permits them to touch and to examine his wounds. Then, as he continues to talk, men come among the cattle and shoot him. The mother says that she doubts the shooting will ever be understood; argument still persists whether it was done to end his suffering or to silence his message.

Now, as at the beginning of the story, we have a long series of questions and answers, mostly having to do with the message The One Who Came Back had brought. At first the mother says that he *"must* have been out of his mind," but finally she divulges what he is reported to have said. *"Each one is himself . . . Not of the herd. . . . Obey nobody. . . . Break down the fences. . . . For if even a few do not hear me, or disbelieve me, we are all betrayed. . . . Let those who can, kill Man. Let those who cannot, avoid him. . . . So long as Man holds dominion over us . . . bear no young."* And the mother says that far out on the range still live some "very old ones, who have never been taken" and who come together "to talk and just to think . . . about the heroism and the terror of two sublime Beings, The One Who Came Back, and The Man With The Hammer."

The mother then tries to disarm this legend by saying it is only something "to frighten children with." But in the last few sentences of the story we learn that she has failed to frighten the young one who dreams of the day he shall "charge . . . The Man With The Hammer" and "put Him and His Hammer out of the way forever," and we learn too that she has failed to make the story clear to the youngest, who whispers the question "What's a train?"

The essential Agee ambiguities are here. The mother is right to tell the story, and right to say that it is only a story. The One Who Came Back is right in his heroism and defiance, and The Man With The Hammer is right in his ultimate and final judgment. It is proper to rail and struggle against fate, but fate cannot be avoided. One might even make a parallel here between Oedipus and The One Who Came Back To Be Shot: to try to avoid one's fate is sin. The Man With The Hammer will not be gainsaid.

And here also is what at least one critic has taken to be an essential part of the Agee style, the use of the narrator's eye as a camera that pans back and forth and booms in and out. Such a technique was perhaps inevitable. "A Mother's Tale" was written at about the same time as was a television script on the life of Abraham Lincoln, when Agee was nearing the end of a distinguished career as a critic of the movies and a writer of scripts, and two years after he had written in an essay on the work of John Huston that the movie was "the greatest art medium of [the] century." Agee was, in fact, more involved and for a longer time in the movies than in any other form of art. While in his first job at *Fortune* he produced his earliest scripts. During much of the time between 1941 and 1948 he was *Time*'s movie critic, and from 1942 to 1948 he wrote his famous column about the movies for the *Nation*.

Perhaps the first record of this interest in the movies dates from 1930 when Agee wrote for the Harvard *Advocate* a review of *God's Man: A Novel in Wood Cuts* by Lynd Ward, a book that he says "could certainly never have existed, but for the movies." The review is blandly undergraduate in tone. Without argument or evidence it makes easy distinctions between good directors and conventional artists. It labels Murnau's *Sunrise* "one of the best movies ever made." And it argues that although *God's Man* is a "ham narrative" it is "ideally suited to the author's chosen medium," apparently meaning that the artist and his medium are more important than what the artist says, that personality and manner are more important than message.

In Agee's more mature criticism this easy personalism obtrudes from time to time. He was always to put his close attention upon the film under examination, but he was rarely to view it in the light of any formal theory or standard. In his first piece for the *Nation* Agee described himself as an amateur who was "deeply interested in moving pictures, considerably experienced from childhood on in watching them and thinking and talking about them, and totally, or almost totally, without experience or even much secondhand knowledge of how they are made." And he said that "it would be a question entirely of the maturity of my judgment, and not in the least of my professional or amateur standing, whether I were right or wrong" about the pictures he would review.

This "amateur subjectivism" makes him a difficult man to pin down. He often took refuge in adjectives like "false" and "wooden" and "real." And he sometimes came close to falling into what later became the "camp" trap. About the film version of *To Have and Have Not,* for instance, he wrote that it showed "a kidding appreciation of honky-tonk," was "specious," but that he had a "weakness" for this kind of thing. He could, on the other hand, wax fairly eloquent about these campy things. "The best of [the picture] had for me at least a little of the nostalgia of highballs that taste like rotten mahogany, defective mechanical pianos at implacable fortissimo, or gents-rooms strangled with the fragrance of mentholated raspberries." "Mainly subjective" of course this is, as he was to admit openly in an essay on D. W. Griffith.

Although he was aware of his subjectivism, and perhaps because he was so aware, he wrote many reviews filled with what might be called either hedges and evasions or honest attempts to be unbiased and objective. A picture condemned for being "boyscoutish in its social attitudes" would be praised for having attitudes, condemned for having photography that "goes velvety" but praised for having photography that "earnestly" strives for a "real, not a false, attitude." Perhaps his most readable criticism, therefore, is almost purely descriptive. He explains John Huston's direction by describing the picture or the scene. And one of the high points in his famous nostalgic essay "Comedy's Greatest Era" is a long description of the way in which Buster Keaton and the girl pursue and finally find each other in *The Navigator*; to read it is almost as much fun as to watch the movie.

During his career as critic, Agee saw the Great Depression give way to the New Deal, and World War II followed by the era of Senator Joseph McCarthy. Events shaped the movies of the time, and Agee spoke out both about the movies and about the events. He did not dodge political issues. He doubted that "the politicians of [any] camp" could "supply me, the world in general, or even their closest associates, with the truth. . . . I am immobilized . . . by my conviction that a primary capacity for telling or discovering the truth is possible, today, to few human beings in few types of occupation or allegiance." In the face of these doubts, it may have been naive for Agee to argue that certain films of certain kinds would be instrumental in bringing truth to the people of the United States. Even when he knew that many of the movies produced were either outright propaganda or rank escapism, he continued to express the hope that truthful films would be produced, that they would explain the way things actually were. During the war he saw the United States as suffering "a unique and constantly intensifying schizophrenia. . . . Those Americans who are doing the fighting are doing it in parts of the world which seem irrelevant to them . . . This chasm widens and deepens daily between our fighting and civilian populations. . . . Their experience of war is unprecedented in immediacy and unanimity. Ours . . . is essentially specialized, lonely, bitter, and sterile; our great majority will emerge from war almost as if it had never taken place." He pleaded therefore that the documentary films from the fighting fronts be released. To his readers he said, "I can only urge you to write your Congressman, if he can read."

But his sense of involvement with his fellow men later led him to almost the opposite view. In 1945 he wrote that he was "beginning to believe that, for all that may be said in favor of our seeing these terrible records of war, we have no business seeing this sort of experience except through our presence and participation. . . . Pornography is invariably degrading to anyone who looks at or reads it. If at an incurable distance from participation, hopelessly incapable of reactions adequate to the event, we watch men killing each other, we may be quite as profoundly degrading ourselves and, in the process, betraying and separating ourselves the farther from those we are trying to identify ourselves with."

Obviously, Agee was during these years developing a deep awareness of social and economic and moral problems. He was so moved by the moral implications of Chaplin's *Monsieur Verdoux* that he devoted three of his *Nation* columns to the picture. In part because Chaplin dealt with a man who murdered women in order to support his crippled wife and his son, *Verdoux* was not generously received by those who thought they knew what Chaplin *should* have done. But Agee wrote that Chaplin's theme was "the greatest and the most appropriate to its time that he has yet undertaken" — "the bare problem of surviving at all in such a world as this. . . . [Ver-

18

doux] has made the assumption that most people make, today — one of the chief assumptions on which modern civilization rests. That is, that in order to preserve intact in such a world as this those aspects of the personality which are best and dearest to one, it is necessary to exercise all that is worst in one . . . When the worst and the best in the personality are . . . segregated, and the worst is . . . utilized in the nominal service of the best, it is inevitably the good which is exploited; the evil, which thinks of itself as faithful slave, is treacherous master; and evil, being active and knowledgeable, grows; and good, rendered motionless and denied knowledge, withers."

That was written in 1947, in June. By December even colder winds were blowing, with Hollywood writers and others being cited for contempt by Congress and even being fired by their employers. "I believe that a democracy which cannot contain all its enemies, of whatever kind or virulence, is finished as a democracy. . . . It seems to me that the mere conception of a vigorous and genuine democracy . . . depends on a capacity for faith in human beings so strong that on its basis one can dare to assume that goodness and intelligence will generally prevail over stupidity and evil. This is, I would presume, the bravest and noblest faith of which men . . . are capable; but I cannot see that this faith is any longer available . . . It seems to me that virtually nobody, any more, chooses even to try to honor and trust even himself, or even his best potentialities. Failing that, it is of course impossible to deal honorably or trustworthily with others; and we have harrowing evidence what a peculiarly infernal mechanism democracy inevitably becomes when it is manipulated by and for people who no longer understand its meaning and purpose."

By 1950 Agee had begun to "preach" and to argue about the camera in moral terms also. In his essay on John Huston he deplored Huston's having become a "camera" man. The camera "should not impose on the story." True, this might be read as a purely aesthetic argument, but what we have seen of the development of Agee's thought indicates that it is more. His argument, of course, was not that the camera should be static or undirected. In fact his very first script, as did his last, contained directions for the camera so precise and so explicit that a director, in shooting the script, could if he desired be simply a taker of direction.

Agee's earliest script, "Notes for a Moving Picture: The House," is not a standard script but rather the description, almost frame by frame, of a completed picture. It anticipates the "modern" film in many ways. It calls for the use of color and black and white in the same frame. It echoes Dada with neon signs that "spell out not real sign-words but semi-intelligible or international names and nouns for suspense and disaster." Its characters appear out of nowhere and sometimes disappear "ten feet in front of the camera." One of them is distinguished by a "swinging penis nose." One woman wears a corsage in the form of an "exhausted phallus" that two pages later turns into the head of a Pekinese dog and finally goes to sleep.

"The House" deals symbolically with the rise of Hitlerism and with a decadent family whose selfishness and egocentricity might be inferred to be among the causes or results of fascism. It ends with the destruction of that family's big house in a great storm of wind and rain, when a group of "very poor children" come upon the scene and one of the girls finds "a film of drowned lace curtain" and a boy picks up a derby. In the closing shot "only the bride in the curtain, the groom in the derby, remain," apparently heirs to a ruined and devastated civilization.

Agee makes certain that we know just what the camera is doing. "For as long as three minutes the camera is absolutely stationary: then, first with flickerlike flashes and later with a more jabbing and steady rhythm, the basic position-one shot is crosslanced (not in double exposure) with swift intimate detail of childish feet grinding faces of Negroes, Jews; a heel twisting out the lenses of horn-rimmed spectacles; a little hand grabbing at an open book and ripping out leaves (blood springs after); hands (childish) belaboring drums, cymbals." At one point the camera "settles gently to rest in the dark front hallway before an ornate hatrack and looks at itself close and hard in the mirror, beginning very softly to purr (the reduced dry sound of its motor); swings back to center of hall, beneath center of stairwell, and delicately takes flight" to resume its normal function, the observer seeing again not the camera but what the camera sees.

"The House" was never filmed. Nor was Agee's second script, "Man's Fate — A Film Treatment of the Malraux Novel," which was also a described picture rather than a formal shooting script. In this manner too and never filmed was a later satire, "Dedication Day," first published in 1946. Of all the scripts, only "The House" and "Dedication Day" were original compositions. The rest were based on novels, *The African Queen* and *The Night of the Hunter*, on Stephen Crane short stories, "The Bride Comes to Yellow Sky" and "The Blue Hotel," and on the journal of Paul Gauguin, *Noa Noa*.

In all of them, however, Agee paid careful attention to the camera's precisely defined function. But no matter how carefully he outlined the process of filming, he wanted the result to look not like a movie but like reality. (He frequently called for the use of orthochromatic film, for grainy film, for the look of the newsreel.) In the scripts one may see the aesthetic and philosophic dilemma that arose on the one hand from Agee's doubts about the validity or importance of art and on the other hand from his feeling that the artist is better and more important than the ordinary man.

For example, to "Man's Fate" he appended a set of "Notes" in which he explained what he hoped would happen when the direc tor came to manage the chorus of offstage voices called for in the script. "The problem would be to find the right voices — entirely untrained, un'cultivated' and above all unhistrionic . . ." He wrote similarly that "various head-groupings, faces, etc., would not be 'composed' and romantic but literalness intensified to become formal out of its own substance." It is as if art were inferior to actuality, and the artist incapable of achieving anything as beautiful as the material he uses. The "untrained" is raised to the level of Keats's "unheard."

In one of the last things he ever wrote, however, the script for *Noa Noa*, he spoke up for the artist, apparently having decided that even though art might be at its best when it looked the least like art it still had to be made by the artist. In writing this script he was himself the most self-conscious of artists. To a portrayal of the funeral of the last Maori king he devoted four pages showing brilliant virtuosity and laid out note by note and frame by frame a scripting in which medium shots and long shots and cuts are synchronized with the beating of the drums, sometimes calling for eight shots to a beat and working up to "a series of fluttering shots . . . so similar in frame that, at this fluttering speed, they form a composite."

The central character is Paul Gauguin, standing alone, fighting against civilization and the government, overcoming disease and pain, struggling to his artistic apotheosis despite drug addiction and even blindness. The script opens and closes with scenes in which the artist, if not quite equated with, is at least compared with Jesus Christ. And at one point in the story, one of Gauguin's Tahitian friends says to him, "You give men everything, beyond their just staying alive. You make them know that it is a great wonder to be alive; a great joy; a mystery and fear; an honor." The man who gives man "everything" is the absolutely revolutionary anti-establishment artist, who gives even though he is destroyed by those to whom he gave, and abandoned by his friends.

W. M. Frohock, writing about Agee and "the question of wasted talent," seems to agree with the doctrine of art's sacredness, but he thinks that Agee did not live by the doctrine. "The truth is that with all the different possibilities open, [Agee] did not want to choose one and put the rest aside." This Frohock blames on America, which "invites talent to disperse." He argues that Agee was deficient as an artist (or less significant than he might have been) because he did not make the kind of choice that Paul Gauguin made.

Evidence exists that Agee himself sometimes feared he had not made the proper choices. It is even possible that he punished himself for his nonmessianic behavior. John Huston says that Agee "held his body in very slight regard altogether, feeding it with whatever was at hand, allowing it to go to sleep when there was nothing else for it to do, begrudging it anything beneficial such as medicine when he was sick. On the other hand, he was a chain smoker and a bottle-a-night man. . . . His body destruction was implicit in his make-up."

David Cornel DeJong tells of an evening with Agee. This was in the 1930's, when DeJong's "income from writing amounted to all of two thousand dollars a year" and when Agee was preparing to go to Alabama on the *Fortune* assignment that resulted eventually in *Let Us Now Praise Famous Men*. It was "an evening of . . . smoke. . . . Somewhere along the way I got a pretty clear idea about the definite figures, money figures, Agee and Evans were to receive from their labors for *Fortune* . . . a sum roughly seven times greater than I was earning annually. The great rue of being made to perpetrate what they were perpetrating eluded me. The envy of others present didn't. After I left and had already reached the street, Jim Agee opened a window and shouted down to me:

'DeJong, don't you dare sell your soul and guts. You have them for free, keep them so.' All things are relative and it isn't even fair to take this Agee text out of context. But wasn't he actually asking me to hold on to my free soul and guts because if I didn't I might be inducing him and others like him to become more mournful? No, I wasn't romantic enough, and I badly lacked a sense of gainful social consciousness. I was such an integral part of it I couldn't afford to step outside of it and look down upon it with anger and remorse."

Some bitterness is evident here and some anger. But clearly De-Jong saw a difference between his way of living — by writing when he could write and by publishing when he could publish and in the intervals of financial or creative dryness taking manual-labor jobs — and the Agee way of living and writing. The great Agee difficulty, what DeJong calls rue, lay perhaps in Agee's attempts to use the establishment, or at least to work inside it, while coming to an increasingly acute awareness of its great failings and its essential ungodliness.

Agee described his years on the staff of *Fortune* from two viewpoints. As a student he had written that "nothing gives me more delight than getting hold of . . . a question that I've really read up on and 'writing myself dry' on it." While at *Fortune* it was still true that "no other earthly thing is as important . . . as learning how to write." But at the same time he was living through "three years of exposure to foulness through *Fortune* and the general News" that were to lead him into "cynicism" and almost into communism. As for communism, "there are things about it I despise. But there are things all through the world that look to me bad, and there are many things in that set of ideas which look to me good."

He wrote for *Fortune* articles about the Mohawk Carpet Mills and about TVA. The editor-in-chief "was much impressed" by the TVA article and proposed that Agee learn more about "the business ropes." Agee replied that he would "work as hard and as much as possible." The big thing was to learn to write — about anything. But he was, alas, learning in a world that was coming apart at the seams. The article on the carpet mills was followed in the same issue of the magazine by an article on "Germany's Reichswehr." And Agee wrote a series of captions for a set of Bourke-White photographs from the dust bowl of middle America. He also wrote an article on modern furniture and one on "The U.S. Commercial Orchid," of which he wrote to Father Flye that "people's reactions to [the flower] have been and are so vile that I hate its very guts along with theirs."

In November of 1935 Agee had saved enough money to get away from *Fortune* for a time. He spent almost six months in Anna Maria, Florida, during which time he was to write, among other things, a remarkable letter to Father Flye. He had learned that "things have to be believed with the body or in other words soul, not just perceived of the mind." He had learned that "I care mainly about just 2 things. . . . They would be (1) getting as near truth and whole truth as is humanly possible . . . and (2) setting this (near-) truth out in the clearest and cleanest possible terms." Standing between him and these ends was "a pretty strong undertone of cold fear or despair." This is the letter that contains the description of his "cynicism" and also the argument about communism.

In June of 1936 Agee was back in New York. *Fortune* assigned him to go to Alabama with the photographer Walker Evans "to do a story on: A sharecropper family (daily & yearly life): and also a study of Farm Economics in the South (impossible for me): and also on the several efforts to help the situation: i.e. Govt. and state work; theories & wishes of Southern liberals . . ." This assignment he called the "best break I ever had on *Fortune*." And he felt a "terrific personal responsibility" toward the story, but he had "considerable doubts" of his ability to "bring it off" and "considerable more of *Fortune*'s ultimate willingness to use it as it seems (in theory) to me."

Agee moved with Evans into the South, planning on "a month's work," but actually staying for eight weeks. In September he wrote to Father Flye from New York that the trip had been "very hard," but still "one of the best things I've ever had happen to me." At the time of writing this, Agee was at work on putting his material into shape for *Fortune*, but he was finding it very difficult and was afraid that in trying to fit what he had into the *Fortune* formula he was losing his "ability to make it right in my own way." In the end, *Fortune*, under a new editor, decided not to use the material at all.

It was five years before the Alabama story found its way into print. When it appeared, as *Let Us Now Praise Famous Men*, *Time*'s reviewer called it "a distinguished failure." The book is both a piece of reportage and an agonizing self-examination by a Puritan who both despised and was "sized" by Puritanism, a mystic divided against himself and still struggling with problems that had first occupied him in boyhood, who could not believe in psychoanalysis "enough to subject myself to it," and who trusted only "a feeling of God, and love, and in part myself." The book demands, as few other books do, a reading in the light of the writer's own life. Agee, for instance, in October of 1937, made application a second time for a Guggenheim Fellowship, listing almost fifty projects to which he said he would like to devote his energies. Among the projects was something he called "An Alabama Record," which was to be "as exhaustive a reproduction and analysis of personal experience, including the phases and problems of memory and recall and revisitation and the problems of writing and of communication, as I am capable of, with constant bearing on two points: to tell everything possible as accurately as possible: and to invent nothing. It involves as total a suspicion of 'creative' and 'artistic' as of 'reportorial' attitudes and methods, and it is likely therefore to involve the development of some more or less new forms of writing and of observation. . . . One part of the work, in many senses the crucial part, would be a strict comparison of the photographs and the prose as relative liars and relative reproducers of the same matters." The application was rejected, perhaps because its scope and variety and brilliance made the Guggenheim authorities think of a fireworks factory ablaze on a dark and windy night, and perhaps because Agee's obvious desire to see and to report everything led him to describe his "anti-Communist manifesto" first in terms of an "assumption and statement . . . of belief in ideas and basic procedures of Communism" before he moved on to the "anti" part that was to deal with "misconceptions, corruptions, misuses" and all the rest.

Agee was able, however, to obtain a small advance from a publisher. He retired to Frenchtown, New Jersey, to work on what was then called *Three Tenant Families.* It was difficult both financially and spiritually. He could not write as well or as quickly as he wanted. He was troubled by what he called "a form of inverted snobbery . . . an innate and automatic respect and humility toward all who are very poor and toward all the unassuming and non-pompous who are old," and he saw the book as a "piece of spiritual burglary." When it finally appeared in 1941 and Father Flye had written to him about it, Agee responded, "What you write of the book needless to say is good to hear to the point of shaming me — for it is a sinful book at least in all degrees of 'falling short of the mark' and I think in more corrupt ways as well."

The corruption was not quite of a piece with the *Fortune* "foulness." *Fortune,* of course, during the years of Agee's association, had been staffed by men at least some of whom did not believe that business was America's primary business. Because of the biases of these men, and the terror of the times, *Fortune* ran stories about strikers and men on relief alongside articles about "Mr. Rockefeller's $14,000,000 Idyl" at Williamsburg. A "Success Story" bore the subtitle "The Life and Circumstances of Mr. Gerald Corkum — Paint Sprayer in the Plymouth Motor Plant [or] How to Own Your Own Home on $1,200 a Year, Which You Are Not Sure of Making." Even families on relief were dealt with in these terms; Steve Hatalla was considered significant by *Fortune* because, although he had "lost his job four years ago" his family of six had lived since then "on $50 a month, or $100 per year per person."

Some of this was "foulness," but the "corruption" was something deeper. In *Let Us Now Praise Famous Men*, Agee explained. In one of the early pages of his book Agee writes: "It seems to me curious, not to say obscene and thoroughly terrifying, that it could occur to an association of human beings drawn together . . . for profit . . . to pry intimately into the lives of an undefended and appallingly damaged group of human beings . . . for the purpose of parading the nakedness, disadvantage and humiliation of these lives before another group of human beings, in the name of science, of 'honest journalism' . . . of humanity, of social fearlessness, for money, and for a reputation for crusading and for unbias . . . and that these people could be capable of meditating this prospect without the slightest doubt of their qualification to do an 'honest' piece of work . . . It seems curious, further, that the assignment of this work should have fallen to persons having so extremely different a form of respect for the subject, and responsibility toward it, that from the first and inevitably they counted their employers . . . among their most dangerous enemies."

Although that paragraph is aimed primarily at *Fortune*, its editors and owners — part of the Luce empire — a reading of the first section of his book soon shows that Agee was thinking of *Fortune* as a symptom or symbol of a deeper corruption, a more serious problem. His deepest doubts concerned the function of any writer, whether or not he worked for *Fortune*, and the possibility that unhuman feelings of superiority can arise in any man calling himself "writer" or even "reporter." In this book we see Agee worrying about a division in his own soul, a division more tragic than any of the standard accepted divisions between rich and poor, scab and striker.

Of course, large parts of the book show that when Agee and Evans found their assigned tenant farmers they went about their journalistic job with dispatch and precision. In typical Luce-man fashion they catalogued the contents of the rooms in the farmhouses, of the drawers in the chests. They described carefully the clothing of their subjects even to the manner in which overalls wrinkle. They moved furniture in order to get pictures that would effectively show what the tenant family house was like; the bed that is described as "directly opposite this partition door" and standing with "its foot . . . just short of the kitchen door" was moved crossways for an angle shot. Perhaps this proves that the use of photographs and matching texts is practically impossible. For instance, in another section of the report, oilcloth on a kitchen table is described as "worn thin and through at the corners and along the edges of the table and along the ridged edges of boards in the table surface, and in one or two places, where elbows have rested a great deal . . . rubbed through in a wide hole"; the photograph makes the oilcloth look shiny and nearly unworn, only wrinkled a little here and there, with a small hole where it creases at the table's edge.

This part of the job, the prying and the semblance of "unbias," gave Agee the deepest pain and forced him into the gravest self-examination. And his account of this self-examination and his description of his pain make this book something entirely apart from the usual reporter-photographer collaboration in a piece of journalism. At one point he describes how he catalogues the contents of a house while the occupants are away and then, when he hears them returning, "the innocence of their motions in the rear of the hall," he writes: "I am seated on the front porch with a pencil and an open notebook, and I get up and go toward them. In some bewilderment, they yet love me, and I, how dearly, them; and trust me, despite hurt and mystery, deep beyond making of such a word as trust. It is not going to be easy to look into their eyes."

That he loves them, that he sees great beauty in them and in their lives, leads him to see that these houses "approximate, or at times by chance achieve, an extraordinary 'beauty' " and that "the beauty of a house, inextricably shaped as it is in an economic and human abomination, is at least as important a part of the fact as the abomination itself: but that one is qualified to insist on this only in proportion as one faces . . . the brunt of the meanings, against human beings, of the abomination itself." To write of "economic abomination" would of course offend *Fortune*'s editors, but to Agee this possible offense was of less consequence than his own falling into the "sin" of "feeling in the least apologetic for perceiving the beauty of the houses." He understood the economic causes, was struggling to find his way beyond them, or through them, to the human souls that were afflicted and injured by those causes. He was seeking humanity in inhumanity.

In trying to avoid the sin of feeling apologetic, Agee devotes long pages to an argument about the " 'chance' beauty of 'irrelevances' " and about the intellectual justification for his deep feeling that "the partition wall of the Gudgers' front bedroom *IS* importantly, among other things, a great tragic poem." This leads him of course to something he does not like to admit, that journalism because it exists is as "true" as the wall. Therefore he argues beyond this, that even though "journalism is true in the sense that everything is true," it must be despised for "its own complacent delusion, and its enormous power to poison the public with the same delusion, that it is telling the truth even of what it tells of," and he argues then by analogy that literary "naturalism" is ineffective and sinful unless the writer brings it "level in value at least to music and poetry" and makes certain that his "representation of 'reality' does not sag into, or become one with, naturalism."

This argument is not easy to follow, but we have no doubt that it arises from a love for the people he is writing about. He sees himself as belonging to a world they do not know, a world bent on destroying them. When a group of singers perform for him he is "sick in the knowledge they felt they were here at our demand." When he comes upon a young Negro couple on the road and realizes he has frightened them, he feels that "the least I could have done was to throw myself flat on my face and embrace and kiss their feet." And when he stops himself, describing feelings that recall the early letters about suicide, it is "exactly and as scarcely as you snatch yourself from jumping from a sheer height." He feels "humble, and respectful" and is "careful that I should not so much as set my foot in this clay in a cheapness of attitude, and full of knowledge, I have no right, here, I have no real right, much as I want it, and could never earn it, and should I write of it, must defend it against my kind."

This leads to "the most intense . . . nearly insane . . . frustrations." At times he feels that to show his love for these people he would have to share their lives and experience their sufferings. He wants himself, actually, to be punished. At one time he wishes, in a dirty lunchroom, that the "three hard-built, crazy-eyed boys of eighteen," who looked at him "with immediate and inevitable enmity," would "for their sake and mine" start a fight. At another he has an urgent desire to expose himself, as he feels in his work he is exposing others, and from a bug-ridden bed in a tenant farmer's house he walks out naked into the night. "The instant I was out under the sky, I felt much stronger than before, lawless and lustful to be naked, and at the same time weak. I watched the house and felt like a special sort of burglar; but still more I felt as if I trod

31

water in a sea whose floor was drooped unthinkably deep beneath me, and I was unsafely far from the wall of the ship." Then he goes back to the bugs that they may eat of him. "I don't exactly know why anyone should be 'happy' under these circumstances, but . . . I was: outside the vermin, my senses were taking in nothing but a deep-night unmeditatable consciousness of a world which was newly touched and beautiful to me." And at still another time he watches preparations for breakfast in the Ricketts house. The beauty of the people and of their lives puts him in a sacramental mood and he recalls how as "a child in the innocence of faith" he had got "out of bed . . . to serve at the altar at earliest lonely Mass."

Such an experience is the foundation for *The Morning Watch*, a short novel first published in 1951, ten years after *Let Us Now Praise Famous Men*. The story is simple. It tells of one night in the life of the twelve-year-old Richard whose father had died sometime before and who is now attending an Episcopal school because his mother thinks he needs "to be among other boys." Richard had determined to stay awake during the entire night before Good Friday. But he had fallen asleep and is awakened by a teacher-priest at a quarter of four in the morning to stand his watch before the altar. He performs his religious duties for the first watch and decides to remain in the chapel for a second watch, despite his having been told to come right back to bed. After the second watch, aware that they will be punished anyway, Richard and two of the other boys go swimming in a nearby river and afterward return to the school.

The story is divided into three parts — the awakening, the watches, and the trip to the river and back. The story might be said also to have three major themes: that of the religious struggle in the heart of young Richard; that of his feeling excluded and lonely; that of the growth during the night of his own self-awareness. In the very first paragraph we learn that Richard is disappointed with his religious life, that he has been unable to dedicate himself in the way he thinks he ought. The social theme is also stated early. As the priest comes around to waken the boys we learn about the discipline in the school and we see a good deal of horseplay like the throwing of shoes and hear a good amount of down-to-earth Tennessee profanity and obscenity. Despite the horseplay, Richard has a feeling "something like the feeling . . . he now seldom and faintly recalled, during the morning just after he learned of his father's death." In the second part of the story, the religious and the social again are intertwined. When Richard arrives at the chapel he finds there two older boys who, "alone among the boys now at the School, might have a Vocation." Their job is to trim and change candles and to "remove and replace the withering flowers" on the altar. Richard feels apart from these boys and also from "the great athlete Willard Rivenburg" who is with them but openly irreligious and who "never even crossed himself at a hard time in a game." Richard understands that he has failed; he is not a religious and he is not the athlete whose stance and carriage he has imitated "whenever he had done anything physically creditable." And he knows that his desire not to fail may very well be motivated only by pride.

During the course of the two watches he follows in his mind the events of Good Friday and imagines that he might crucify himself and then rebuke all of the people, his mother, his friends, his teachers, who would ask him to bring himself down from the cross. But the result is only an increased awareness of his pride and, at the end, a sense of frustration. Despite his attempts to torture himself, to assume awkward and painful positions so that his knees and back and arms ache, he whispers to himself, "My cup runneth over," and realizes that "what he saw in his mind's eye was a dry chalice, an empty grail." Ambiguously, "*It is finished*, his soul whispered."

In the third section we see Richard asserting himself and starting down toward the river with the boys surprisingly following him. Again, even though he has apparently achieved one of his ambitions, he thinks that his pride in his success should be condemned. Once in the river, the same self-doubts arise. Richard dives to the bottom and tries to hold himself there. He thinks to himself, "Good. That's fine. *For Thee!*" But then the doubts come again. *"No right! Get out!"* At the surface he consoles himself by thinking *"Anyhow I tried,* meaning at once that he had tried to stay down too long as an act of devotion and that he had tried to save himself from the deadliest of sins." He is a resurrected being. "I could have died, he realized almost casually. *Here I am!* his enchanted body sang." One might argue that "Here I am" is a victory of pride over religious subjection. But one suspects that Agee's sympathy is with Richard and that in the endless struggle between pride and submissiveness, between spirit and flesh, we have a sympathetic account of the struggle through which Agee obviously went during his own life.

The Morning Watch is written in a language that is rich to the point of being almost cloying. Still, the musical complexity in the book is of great importance in the development of the story. We are given, for instance, upon Richard's first entering the chapel, a very long description of the decorations on the altar. Crowds of spring flowers "fainting in vases and jars of metal and glass and clay and in drinking glasses and mason jars and in small and large tin cans," together with the burning candles, make "all one wall of dizzying dazzle." Later, the altar boys come in to put out the "shrunken candles" and to remove from among the flowers those that are dying. Petals fall. Smoke lies upon the air. And when the boy opens the door to bear away the wasted candles, "upon the fragrance of fire and wax . . . there stole the purity of water from a spring." In counterpoint to this long description is one equally long that comes after the boys have left the chapel and started for the river. Going into the woods is to Richard like "leaving a hot morning and stepping into a springhouse." He sees "each separate blossom" of dogwood. He observes the colors of all the tree trunks and the "forms and varieties of bark." The coming of spring is heralded by "mild clouds of blossom" in the "stunned woods." Clearly this is related to Richard's coming out of the river after having plumbed the dark depths and looked upon death. In further counterpoint is Richard's thinking about the death of Christ. After coming out of the river, resurrected, Richard happens upon a snake that has "just struggled out of his old skin" and is full of "cold pride in his new magnificence." He draws his friends' attention to the snake, and one of the boys begins to throw the snake about, flipping him with a long stick. When another boy prepares to kill the snake with a stone, Richard arrests his arm only to realize that he has committed another sin against the society of which he wants to be a part. In expiation he kills the snake, not knowing whether it is poisonous, by hammering it with a stone, "putting his bare hand within range of that clever head." He understands that in his recklessness and brutality he has lost the "contempt" of his friends and could "belong among them if he wanted to." Still, he is not sure that he wants to. He rejects the privilege of carrying the snake back to the school as a sign of his bravery. He reflects upon the fact that the snake will not die before nightfall even though its head is smashed flat. Then, as his friend carries the snake back up the forest path, Richard thinks again of Christ's lingering death — "so hard and so long. It won't be over till sundown." But Richard is "neither surprised nor particularly troubled" when, a few moments later, the boys decide that the snake had best be thrown into the hogpen where it is gobbled down while "its two portions still tingled in the muck."

The major and third theme of the story grows out of the first two. Out of Richard's grapplings with his spiritual problems and out of his anguished attempts to become a part of a society for which he has only small respect (only he and one other boy in the school like to read, for instance) he comes to realize he can take satisfaction even in alienation and exile. This theme is symbolized first during the walk into the woods when he stops to see the shell of a locust with its "hard claws . . . so clenched into the bark that it was only with great care and gentleness that he was able to detach the shell without destroying it." He does remove it, and after examining it very carefully, "with veneration" places it again "in its grip against the rigid bark." Doing this, "he tried to imagine gripping hard enough that he broke his back wide open and pulled himself out of each leg and arm and finger and toe so cleanly and completely that the exact shape would be left intact." He falls behind the other boys and has to hurry to catch up with them and to prepare himself for the rite of diving into the river. Then, on the way back, the snake killed and rejected, he hurries to the tree where he had left the locust shell and removes it "gently" and puts it into his shirt pocket. In the closing paragraphs of the story we see him at first not troubled about the fate of the snake, then full of "horror and pity" because the snake is still alive, and finally understanding that by now the snake was "beyond really feeling anything." This reminds him of his mother's saying that his father at the time of his death had been so "terribly hurt" that God took him "up to Heaven to be with Him." Richard walks back to the school, "his left hand sustaining, in exquisite protectiveness, the bodiless shell which rested against his heart." In the course of his morning watch Richard has learned a great deal, not necessarily about eternal truths but certainly about himself.

An intense desire to know himself marked Agee's work in the three great pieces of sustained prose that lie at the heart of his achievement. In *Let Us Now Praise Famous Men* Agee describes the process by which he came to a new and deep understanding of himself and his world. In *The Morning Watch* he looked back at himself as at the age of twelve he had come to an earlier appreciation of his own identity and importance. In *A Death in the Family* he looks even farther back and exposes the roots from which that twelve-year-old character had grown. And of the three works perhaps the frankest and most revealing is *A Death in the Family*. The young boy who is the central character in this novel is named Rufus, Agee's middle name which was the name he used almost exclusively in signing the letters to Father Flye.

Frohock writes that shortly "before he died Agee told a friend that he needed two months to finish *A Death in the Family*." When the book appeared in 1957, it contained a publisher's note which explained that "the only editorial problem involved the placing of several scenes outside the time span of the basic story. It was finally decided to print these in italics and to put them after Parts I and II." This, the publisher explained, "obviated the necessity of the editors having to compose any transitional material. The short section *Knoxville: Summer of 1915*, which served as a sort of prologue, has been added. It was not a part of the manuscript which Agee left, but the editors would certainly have urged him to include it in the final draft." Whoever they were, the editors produced a very sophisticated and complex work that runs in two streams, the one italicized and the other not, detailing two times of growth in the young Rufus.

The interweaving of these two streams of narrative is accomplished without the use of "modern" psychological tricks. Agee assumes the position of the narrator who understands and explains both of the stories. The tone is set in the very first sentence: "We are talking now of summer evenings in Knoxville, Tennessee in the time that I lived there so successfully disguised to myself as a child." The careful removal of this disguise is the theme of the novel and subsequently of *The Morning Watch* and *Let Us Now Praise Fa-*

mous Men. The three books can be read either in the order of their composition, which would be in the order of Agee's learning about himself, or in the order of their narrative chronology, as an account of the growth of the young Rufus.

This opening Knoxville section establishes the theme and sets the tone. It is a description of an evening of lawn sprinkling and family communion, a description by a mature and intelligent man who is trying to reconstruct his feelings as a small boy. The sophistication of the man's mind can be seen in his remarks about the noises of the locusts. This "is habitual to summer nights, and is of the great order of noises, like the noises of the sea and of the blood her precocious grandchild, which you realize you are hearing only when you catch yourself listening." But more important than physical things, than the observed life of family and neighbors, is the prayer that these matters cause to arise in the mind of the boy after he has been put to bed: "May God bless my people," all those who "quietly treat me, as one familiar and well-beloved" but who "will not, oh, will not, not now, not ever; but will not ever tell me who I am."

Rufus begins to learn something about this in the first non-italicized pages of the novel itself. Rufus' father, Jay Follett, proposes taking the boy to see a Charlie Chaplin movie, and when the mother objects that Chaplin is "nasty" and "vulgar" the father laughs and Rufus feels that the laughter "enclosed him with his father." Jay and Rufus go to the movie, walk home through the dark, stopping twice on the way, first for the father to have two drinks at a saloon, and then on a quiet hillside. During the course of these simple goings on we learn that Rufus is confused by the apparent differences between his mother and his father, that the father has overcome a strong addiction to liquor, and that although the boy feels "enclosed" with his father he still cannot understand him entirely. In the saloon the father lifts Rufus and rests him on the bar and tells all the laughing men that the boy is very bright. This makes Rufus uncomfortable. He has been told many times that "bragging" is a bad thing, and he feels "the anguish of shame" because "you don't brag about smartness if your son is brave."

The story from this point is very simple. The telephone rings in the night and Jay answers it. His brother Ralph is calling to tell him that their father has had a stroke. Although Ralph is not very lucid, Jay decides, from a simple sense of duty and devotion and responsibility, that he will have to drive out into the hills to the family's old home. Returning the next night, having learned that his father is not at death's door, Jay drives fast along the mountain roads. He is anxious to be home by the time he had said he would. A cotter pin wears loose in the steering mechanism of his car, the car goes into the ditch, and Jay is killed instantly by a brain concussion when his chin strikes the steering wheel. The only visible mark of death is a small cut on the chin and a small bruise on the lower lip. The rest of the story tells how Mary, the wife and mother, learns about Jay's death, tells of the arrangements for the funeral and of the funeral itself, and ends a few hours after the burial.

The sub-narrative in the italicized section is equally simple in outline. Rufus wakes up frightened in the night and calls for his father who comes and sings him to sleep. "I hear my father; I need never fear." Rufus' mother has at other times sung to him also. "I hear my mother; I shall never be lonely, or want for love." Rufus learns about the textures of his parent's clothes, about how their cheeks feel, and about how they smell. He discovers after a time of being "aflame with curiosity" that his mother is pregnant. And he is introduced to the problem of race when he asks the majestic black Victoria about her color and says that she smells good. He endures the teasing of his schoolmates who play upon his innocence and trust and who laugh at him after he sings for them as they have asked him to and who tell him that he must be a nigger because he has a nigger's name. With all his family he goes back into the hills to make a call upon his grandfather's grandmother who is over a hundred years old and who recognizes no one but whose "paper mouth" he kisses when ordered and then when "her deep little eyes giggled for joy" he kisses again "with sudden love." And the last part of this sub-narrative is the story of how Rufus goes, again with many members of the family, on a summer trip by train into the Great Smokies. One night at supper when Rufus asks for more cheese "Uncle" Ted, a family friend, says, "Whistle to it and it'll jump off the table into your lap." This precipitates what comes very close to being a family quarrel. Rufus' mother rebukes Ted who retreats by saying it was just a joke and that the boy ought to "learn common sense." Mary is not satisfied and continues to argue that Rufus has "*plenty* of common sense. He's a very bright child *indeed*, if you must know. But he's been brought up to *trust* older people when they tell him something." This of course reminds the reader of the argument that Rufus had with himself earlier about being smart and being brave. The episode ends with Mary still angry and with Jay frowning at her and trying to keep her quiet. This sub-narrative deals in small with the large problem that Rufus faces during the course of the main story about his father's death and burial.

As the sub-narrative weaves in and out of and gives a kind of psychological basis for the main narrative, so within the main narrative do we also have a kind of double vision. Much of what we learn we get through the eyes and the mind of Rufus, but we also learn much that Rufus did not think or see. Large chunks of the story are given us by the humane and intelligent narrator who dwells with loving attention upon the relation of Jay and his wife. While Rufus is asleep and after the telephone call comes to break forever the peace of this little family he describes with great affection how Mary insists upon making breakfast for Jay before he departs, how Jay warms a glass of milk to help Mary go back to sleep after he leaves. He takes almost two pages to describe the noises the automobile makes as it is cranked and starts and moves away down the street, and ends with a kind of E. E. Cummings construction. And finally he tells us how Mary returns to her bed and finds the glass of milk now only tepid, drinks it without pleasure, sees that Jay had drawn the covers up over the bed again but is unaware that he had done it in order to keep the bed warm, for now of course the warmth had all departed.

Rufus and his younger sister are asleep again the next night, when the family gathers after the news has come that Jay is dead. Rufus doesn't hear a long conversation about funeral arrangements, he doesn't hear the family's almost hysterical laughter at a small unintentional joke. And the children are not permitted to attend the funeral itself. But a friend in whose charge they are does permit them to watch the movement of the funeral procession away from the house. Neither does Rufus learn except indirectly about the large conflicts and differences that are described in the main narrative. But the narrator lets the reader see that Mary's father had at first opposed her marriage to Jay, that Mary is devoutly and devotedly religious while her brother and her father are agnostic or nearly atheistic. He also lets us see this difference of opinion against the background of what is really a kind of antagonism between Jay and Mary. The small argument about Charlie Chaplin that opens the novel is paralleled by later small arguments about how much sexual information, for instance, should be given to Rufus. Nor does Rufus understand, except as he had begun to acquire a glimmering understanding in the sub-narrative, the essential split between Mary's and Jay's backgrounds. Mary is intellectual and obviously has some education; she is religious almost to the point of hysterical mysticism; she is quite certain that she knows and can speak to Jay's wandering spirit on the night of his death. Jay, on the other hand, is earthy, has solved that problem of liquor, has at least some liking for the bawdy. He has the manners and habits of the man from the hills and he opposes them to the attitudes of his more urbane wife and her family. Still, and perhaps this too marks him as the man from the hills, he has an absolute and undeviating respect for and allegiance to each and every one of his wife's prejudices.

These differences are suggested in the first chapter about the movie and the walk home, but are made most clear during Jay's drive out into the hills: Jay loves the darkness and the thought of being out in the town at this early morning hour, and he feels very close to the country people who are sleeping in the marketplace awaiting the dawn and a chance to sell their produce. And they are given their most objective correlative when Jay wakes the ferry man, enjoys the feel of the ferry and of the great force in the river, and on the opposite bank meets a hill man and his wife with their mule who have been waiting for the ferry and who will be late for market and so lose their chance for sales. This hill couple is described in great detail and in love, as are their mule and the straining and heaving that accompanies the movement of the wagon down the bank onto the ferry. On the other hand, it is clear that not everything in the hills is good. Jay's brother Ralph is a weakling and a drunkard, and we are given a very long description of the way *he* reacts to his father's illness and to Jay's death and of his own final awareness that he is the "baby," useless, undependable, being thus exposed as the antithesis of Jay and, for that matter, of Mary.

Agee describes these people and these conflicts with unvarying sympathy and with the kind of human acceptance that led him earlier in *Let Us Now Praise Famous Men* to suggest that rather than writing a book he ought to be offering to his audience the actual objects, the food and the excrement, that were parts of the lives of his three tenant families. And it is toward this kind of understanding that Rufus gropes through the main part of *A Death in the Family*. When Mary tells the children about the possibility of their grandfather's death, the conversation turns to the problem of good and evil and in response to the children's questions she says, "We just have to be sure that God knows best. . . . *God — doesn't — believe — in — the — easy — way*. . . . God wants us to *come* to Him, to *find* Him, the best we can." Rufus, of course, is baffled by this. Nor does he comprehend why he should not be permitted to go to school the day after his father's death, why he should not be allowed to go into the streets to tell the passersby that his father is dead. He is puzzled when the priest, come to conduct the funeral service, scolds him and his sister for staring at him. But he feels the presence of death when he rubs his finger around the inside of his father's ashtray and tastes the blackness. And at the end he is confused and hurt by his conversation, after the funeral, with his uncle Andrew.

Andrew takes Rufus for a walk in order to explain what had happened at the burial. Andrew finally says, "If anything makes me believe in God. . . . Or life after death. . . . It'll be what happened this afternoon." And he explains how as the coffin began to lower into the ground "a perfectly magnificent butterfly" settled on it, "just barely making his wings breathe, like a heart." Then, as the coffin reached the bottom of the grave, the sun came out and the butterfly flew "straight up into the sky, so high I couldn't even see him any more." Rufus is moved by this. "He could see it very clearly, because his uncle saw it so clearly when he told about it." But he also sees very clearly that Andrew is angry because the priest insisted upon being called *Father* Jackson and even more angry because Father Jackson had been unable to read the complete burial service. "They call themselves Christians. Bury a man who's a hundred times the man *he'll* ever be, in his stinking, swishing black petticoats, and a hundred times as good a man too, and 'No, there are certain requests and recommendations I cannot make Almighty God for the repose of this soul, for he never stuck his head under a holy-water tap.' "

Rufus is troubled; Andrew, who had a moment before been speaking with great love, is now speaking with hate. He decides that Andrew hates Mary, but he is also sure that he doesn't *really* hate her. He remembers "how many ways [Andrew] had shown how fond he was of" his mother and his family, and he wishes he could ask his uncle, "Why do you hate Mama?" But he doesn't. And the walk, which completes the pattern begun when Jay and Rufus had walked from the movies, continues. "His uncle did not speak except to say, after a few minutes, 'It's time to go home,' and all the way home they walked in silence."

Whether this novel is considered the capstone of the career or a description of the first steps in a long-continuing search for certainty, it is one of the most important things that Agee wrote. It has been compared on the one hand to the work of the young James Joyce and on the other it has been pointed to as proof that Agee should have devoted himself exclusively to what he always called "his own work" rather than skittering about and fooling with things like the movies and criticism. But, whatever our opinion on this matter might be, it seems clear that Agee did during his life what he wanted to do. As early as 1931 he wrote to Father Flye about his good friends the Saunderses, a family that had befriended him and had a large influence upon his development. Agee wrote, "Inevitably barring one's own family, they're the most beautiful and most happy to know and watch, I'd ever seen. . . . Mr. Saunders is something like my grandfather, with the bitterness and unhappiness removed, but with the same calm, beauty and fortitude. I don't know how brilliant a man he might have been, if he'd grimly fought out one of his talents (music most likely, or painting): at any rate, he evidently decided, when he was quite young, not to try it: rather, to work calmly and hard, but with no egoism, on *all* the things he cared most about — and he's resolved his life into the most complete and genuine happiness." Such, one hopes, was the life of James Agee. He was married three times and had four children. His friends and his letters have described how he struggled against and enjoyed liquor and tobacco, how he neglected to have his teeth repaired, how he wore old suits, how he abused his body rather than took care of it, and how during the last years of his life he suffered many severe and painful heart attacks. And the work produced during this life proves that he must have achieved some "genuine happiness."

When Father Flye arrived at the Agee house after Agee's death he found on the mantle in the living room a letter addressed but never mailed. Among other things it contained a long argument about cruelty to animals and, perhaps related to that, a scheme for a movie about elephants. Agee had closed the letter by writing, "Almost nobody I've described it to likes this idea, except me. It has its weaknesses, but I like it. I hope you do."

✦ Selected Bibliography

Works of James Agee

BOOKS

Permit Me Voyage. New Haven, Conn.: Yale University Press, 1934.

Let Us Now Praise Famous Men (with Walker Evans). Boston: Houghton Mifflin, 1941. (Reprinted with an essay and additional photographs by Walker Evans, in 1960.)

The Morning Watch. Boston: Houghton Mifflin, 1951.

A Death in the Family. New York: McDowell, Obolensky, 1957.

Agee on Film: Reviews and Comments. New York: McDowell, Obolensky, 1958.

Agee on Film: Five Film Scripts. New York: McDowell, Obolensky, 1960.

Letters of James Agee to Father Flye. New York: Braziller, 1962.

The Collected Poems of James Agee, edited and with an Introduction by Robert Fitzgerald. Boston: Houghton Mifflin, 1968.

The Collected Short Prose of James Agee, edited and with a Memoir by Robert Fitzgerald. Boston: Houghton Mifflin, 1968.

SHORT PROSE

"Sheep and Shuttleworths," *Fortune*. 7:43 (January 1933).

"T.V.A.," *Fortune*, 11:93 (May 1935).

"Europe: Autumn Story," *Time*, 61:24 (October 15, 1945).

"Religion and the Intellectuals," *Partisan Review*, 17:106 (February 1950).

"A Word or Two about the Author," *Esquire*, 60:149 (December 1969).

"Essay," in *A Way of Seeing* by Helen Levitt. New York: Viking, 1965.

"A Walk before Mass," *Harvard Advocate Centennial Anthology*, edited by Jonathan D. Culler. Cambridge, Mass.: Schenkman, 1966.

"The Silver Sheet," *Harvard Advocate Centennial Anthology*, edited by Jonathan D. Culler. Cambridge, Mass.: Schenkman, 1966.

CURRENT AMERICAN REPRINTS

Agee on Film: Five Film Scripts. Boston: Beacon Press. $2.95.

Agee on Film: Reviews and Comments. Boston: Beacon Press. $2.95.

Collected Poems of James Agee, The. New Haven, Conn.: Yale University Press. $1.75.

Death in the Family, A. New York: Bantam. $.95.

46

Selected Bibliography

Let Us Now Praise Famous Men. New York: Ballantine. $1.25.

Morning Watch, The. New York: Ballantine. $.95.

Critical and Biographical Studies

Barker, George. "Three Tenant Families," *Nation*, 153:282 (September 27, 1941).

Bluestone, George. *Novels into Film*. Baltimore: Johns Hopkins, 1957.

Breit, Harvey. "Cotton Tenantry," *New Republic*, 105:348 (September 15, 1941).

Croce, Arlene. "Hollywood the Monolith," *Commonweal*, 69:430 (January 23, 1959).

DeJong, David Cornel. "Money and Rue," *Carleton Miscellany*, 6:50 (Winter 1965).

Deutsch, Babette. "The Poet as Social Philosopher," *Survey Graphic*, 24:134 (March 1935).

Evans, Walker. "James Agee in 1936," *Atlantic Monthly*, 206:74 (July 1960). Reprinted in 1960 edition of *Let Us Now Praise Famous Men*.

Fitzgerald, Robert. Introduction to *The Collected Poems of James Agee*. Boston: Houghton Mifflin, 1968.

————. "A Memoir," in *The Collected Short Prose of James Agee*. Boston: Houghton Mifflin, 1968.

Frohock, W. H. *The Novel of Violence in America*. Dallas: Southern Methodist University Press, 1950.

Gregory, Horace. Review of *Permit Me Voyage*, *Poetry*, 46:48 (April 1935).

Grossman, James. "Mr. Agee and the *New Yorker*," *Partisan Review*, 12:112 (Winter 1945).

Holder, Allen. "Encounter in Alabama," *Virginia Quarterly Review*, 42:189 (Spring 1966).

Huston, John. Introduction to *Agee on Film: Five Film Scripts*. New York: McDowell, Obolensky, 1960.

Kazin, Alfred. *On Native Grounds*. New York: Reynal and Hitchcock, 1942.

Larsen, Erling. "Let Us Not Now Praise Ourselves," *Carleton Miscellany*, 2:86 (Winter 1961).

Macdonald, Dwight. *Against the American Grain*. New York: Random House, 1962.

Ohlin, Peter H. *Agee*. New York: Ivan Obolensky, 1966.

Phelps, Robert. "James Agee," in *The Letters of James Agee to Father Flye*. New York: Braziller, 1962.

Thompson, Ralph. Review of *Let Us Now Praise Famous Men*, *New York Times*, August 19, 1941, p. 19.

Updike, John. "No Use Talking," *New Republic*, 147:23 (August 13, 1962).